MW01286094

THIS BOOK BELONGS TO:

_____

_____

_____

WEBSITE
USERNAME
PASSWORD
NOTES

• •

WEBSITE
USERNAME
PASSWORD
NOTES

• •

WEBSITE
USERNAME
PASSWORD
NOTES

• •

WEBSITE
USERNAME
PASSWORD
NOTES

WEBSITE _____
USERNAME _____
PASSWORD _____
NOTES _____
_____
_____

• •

WEBSITE _____
USERNAME _____
PASSWORD _____
NOTES _____
_____
_____

• •

WEBSITE _____
USERNAME _____
PASSWORD _____
NOTES _____
_____
_____

• •

WEBSITE _____
USERNAME _____
PASSWORD _____
NOTES _____
_____
_____

WEBSITE _____

USERNAME _____

PASSWORD _____

NOTES _____

_____

_____

• •

WEBSITE _____

USERNAME _____

PASSWORD _____

NOTES _____

_____

_____

• •

WEBSITE _____

USERNAME _____

PASSWORD _____

NOTES _____

_____

_____

• •

WEBSITE _____

USERNAME _____

PASSWORD _____

NOTES _____

_____

_____

WEBSITE

USERNAME

PASSWORD

NOTES

• •

WEBSITE

USERNAME

PASSWORD

NOTES

• •

WEBSITE

USERNAME

PASSWORD

NOTES

• •

WEBSITE

USERNAME

PASSWORD

NOTES

B

WEBSITE
USERNAME
PASSWORD
NOTES

WEBSITE
USERNAME
PASSWORD
NOTES

WEBSITE
USERNAME
PASSWORD
NOTES

WEBSITE
USERNAME
PASSWORD
NOTES

WEBSITE

USERNAME

PASSWORD

NOTES

• •

WEBSITE

USERNAME

PASSWORD

NOTES

• •

WEBSITE

USERNAME

PASSWORD

NOTES

• •

WEBSITE

USERNAME

PASSWORD

NOTES

B

WEBSITE

USERNAME

PASSWORD

NOTES

. . . .

WEBSITE

USERNAME

PASSWORD

NOTES

. . . .

WEBSITE

USERNAME

PASSWORD

NOTES

. . . .

WEBSITE

USERNAME

PASSWORD

NOTES

WEBSITE

USERNAME

PASSWORD

NOTES

• •

WEBSITE

USERNAME

PASSWORD

NOTES

• •

WEBSITE

USERNAME

PASSWORD

NOTES

• •

WEBSITE

USERNAME

PASSWORD

NOTES

WEBSITE _____
USERNAME _____
PASSWORD _____
NOTES _____
_____
_____

• •

WEBSITE _____
USERNAME _____
PASSWORD _____
NOTES _____
_____
_____

• •

WEBSITE _____
USERNAME _____
PASSWORD _____
NOTES _____
_____
_____

• •

WEBSITE _____
USERNAME _____
PASSWORD _____
NOTES _____
_____
_____

WEBSITE

USERNAME

PASSWORD

NOTES

· ·

WEBSITE

USERNAME

PASSWORD

NOTES

· ·

WEBSITE

USERNAME

PASSWORD

NOTES

· ·

WEBSITE

USERNAME

PASSWORD

NOTES

C

WEBSITE

USERNAME

PASSWORD

NOTES

* *

WEBSITE

USERNAME

PASSWORD

NOTES

* *

WEBSITE

USERNAME

PASSWORD

NOTES

* *

WEBSITE

USERNAME

PASSWORD

NOTES

WEBSITE

USERNAME

PASSWORD

NOTES

··

WEBSITE

USERNAME

PASSWORD

NOTES

··

WEBSITE

USERNAME

PASSWORD

NOTES

··

WEBSITE

USERNAME

PASSWORD

NOTES

D

WEBSITE

USERNAME

PASSWORD

NOTES

• •

WEBSITE

USERNAME

PASSWORD

NOTES

• •

WEBSITE

USERNAME

PASSWORD

NOTES

• •

WEBSITE

USERNAME

PASSWORD

NOTES

WEBSITE
USERNAME
PASSWORD
NOTES

• •

WEBSITE
USERNAME
PASSWORD
NOTES

• •

WEBSITE
USERNAME
PASSWORD
NOTES

• •

WEBSITE
USERNAME
PASSWORD
NOTES

D

WEBSITE

USERNAME

PASSWORD

NOTES

· ·

WEBSITE

USERNAME

PASSWORD

NOTES

· ·

WEBSITE

USERNAME

PASSWORD

NOTES

· ·

WEBSITE

USERNAME

PASSWORD

NOTES

WEBSITE

USERNAME

PASSWORD

NOTES

· ·

WEBSITE

USERNAME

PASSWORD

NOTES

· ·

WEBSITE

USERNAME

PASSWORD

NOTES

· ·

WEBSITE

USERNAME

PASSWORD

NOTES

E

WEBSITE

USERNAME

PASSWORD

NOTES

• •

WEBSITE

USERNAME

PASSWORD

NOTES

• •

WEBSITE

USERNAME

PASSWORD

NOTES

• •

WEBSITE

USERNAME

PASSWORD

NOTES

WEBSITE
USERNAME
PASSWORD
NOTES

● ●

WEBSITE
USERNAME
PASSWORD
NOTES

● ●

WEBSITE
USERNAME
PASSWORD
NOTES

● ●

WEBSITE
USERNAME
PASSWORD
NOTES

E

WEBSITE _____

USERNAME _____

PASSWORD _____

NOTES _____

_____

_____

• •

WEBSITE _____

USERNAME _____

PASSWORD _____

NOTES _____

_____

_____

• •

WEBSITE _____

USERNAME _____

PASSWORD _____

NOTES _____

_____

_____

• •

WEBSITE _____

USERNAME _____

PASSWORD _____

NOTES _____

_____

_____

WEBSITE
USERNAME
PASSWORD
NOTES

• •

WEBSITE
USERNAME
PASSWORD
NOTES

• •

WEBSITE
USERNAME
PASSWORD
NOTES

• •

WEBSITE
USERNAME
PASSWORD
NOTES

F

WEBSITE _____

USERNAME _____

PASSWORD _____

NOTES _____

_____

_____

• •

WEBSITE _____

USERNAME _____

PASSWORD _____

NOTES _____

_____

_____

• •

WEBSITE _____

USERNAME _____

PASSWORD _____

NOTES _____

_____

_____

• •

WEBSITE _____

USERNAME _____

PASSWORD _____

NOTES _____

_____

_____

WEBSITE

USERNAME

PASSWORD

NOTES

・・・・・・・・・・・・・・・・・・・・・・・・・・・・・

WEBSITE

USERNAME

PASSWORD

NOTES

・・・・・・・・・・・・・・・・・・・・・・・・・・・・・

WEBSITE

USERNAME

PASSWORD

NOTES

・・・・・・・・・・・・・・・・・・・・・・・・・・・・・

WEBSITE

USERNAME

PASSWORD

NOTES

F

WEBSITE
USERNAME
PASSWORD
NOTES

● ●

WEBSITE
USERNAME
PASSWORD
NOTES

● ●

WEBSITE
USERNAME
PASSWORD
NOTES

● ●

WEBSITE
USERNAME
PASSWORD
NOTES

WEBSITE

USERNAME

PASSWORD

NOTES

· ·

WEBSITE

USERNAME

PASSWORD

NOTES

· ·

WEBSITE

USERNAME

PASSWORD

NOTES

· ·

WEBSITE

USERNAME

PASSWORD

NOTES

WEBSITE

USERNAME

PASSWORD

NOTES

- -

WEBSITE

USERNAME

PASSWORD

NOTES

- -

WEBSITE

USERNAME

PASSWORD

NOTES

- -

WEBSITE

USERNAME

PASSWORD

NOTES

WEBSITE

USERNAME

PASSWORD

NOTES

· ·

WEBSITE

USERNAME

PASSWORD

NOTES

· ·

WEBSITE

USERNAME

PASSWORD

NOTES

· ·

WEBSITE

USERNAME

PASSWORD

NOTES

G

WEBSITE

USERNAME

PASSWORD

NOTES

· ·

WEBSITE

USERNAME

PASSWORD

NOTES

· ·

WEBSITE

USERNAME

PASSWORD

NOTES

· ·

WEBSITE

USERNAME

PASSWORD

NOTES

WEBSITE

USERNAME

PASSWORD

NOTES

· ·

WEBSITE

USERNAME

PASSWORD

NOTES

· ·

WEBSITE

USERNAME

PASSWORD

NOTES

· ·

WEBSITE

USERNAME

PASSWORD

NOTES

WEBSITE _____
USERNAME _____
PASSWORD _____
NOTES _____
_____
_____

• •

WEBSITE _____
USERNAME _____
PASSWORD _____
NOTES _____
_____
_____

• •

WEBSITE _____
USERNAME _____
PASSWORD _____
NOTES _____
_____
_____

• •

WEBSITE _____
USERNAME _____
PASSWORD _____
NOTES _____
_____
_____

WEBSITE
USERNAME
PASSWORD
NOTES

• •

WEBSITE
USERNAME
PASSWORD
NOTES

• •

WEBSITE
USERNAME
PASSWORD
NOTES

• •

WEBSITE
USERNAME
PASSWORD
NOTES

WEBSITE _____

USERNAME _____

PASSWORD _____

NOTES _____

_____

_____

· ·

WEBSITE _____

USERNAME _____

PASSWORD _____

NOTES _____

_____

_____

· ·

WEBSITE _____

USERNAME _____

PASSWORD _____

NOTES _____

_____

_____

· ·

WEBSITE _____

USERNAME _____

PASSWORD _____

NOTES _____

_____

_____

WEBSITE

USERNAME

PASSWORD

NOTES

• •

WEBSITE

USERNAME

PASSWORD

NOTES

• •

WEBSITE

USERNAME

PASSWORD

NOTES

• •

WEBSITE

USERNAME

PASSWORD

NOTES

I

WEBSITE
USERNAME
PASSWORD
NOTES

• •

WEBSITE
USERNAME
PASSWORD
NOTES

• •

WEBSITE
USERNAME
PASSWORD
NOTES

• •

WEBSITE
USERNAME
PASSWORD
NOTES

WEBSITE

USERNAME

PASSWORD

NOTES

• •

WEBSITE

USERNAME

PASSWORD

NOTES

• •

WEBSITE

USERNAME

PASSWORD

NOTES

• •

WEBSITE

USERNAME

PASSWORD

NOTES

I

WEBSITE _____

USERNAME _____

PASSWORD _____

NOTES _____

_____

_____

• •

WEBSITE _____

USERNAME _____

PASSWORD _____

NOTES _____

_____

_____

• •

WEBSITE _____

USERNAME _____

PASSWORD _____

NOTES _____

_____

_____

• •

WEBSITE _____

USERNAME _____

PASSWORD _____

NOTES _____

_____

_____

WEBSITE _____

USERNAME _____

PASSWORD _____

NOTES _____

_____

_____

• •

WEBSITE _____

USERNAME _____

PASSWORD _____

NOTES _____

_____

_____

• •

WEBSITE _____

USERNAME _____

PASSWORD _____

NOTES _____

_____

_____

• •

WEBSITE _____

USERNAME _____

PASSWORD _____

NOTES _____

_____

_____

J

WEBSITE

USERNAME

PASSWORD

NOTES

• •

WEBSITE

USERNAME

PASSWORD

NOTES

• •

WEBSITE

USERNAME

PASSWORD

NOTES

• •

WEBSITE

USERNAME

PASSWORD

NOTES

WEBSITE

USERNAME

PASSWORD

NOTES

• •

WEBSITE

USERNAME

PASSWORD

NOTES

• •

WEBSITE

USERNAME

PASSWORD

NOTES

• •

WEBSITE

USERNAME

PASSWORD

NOTES

J

WEBSITE _____
USERNAME _____
PASSWORD _____
NOTES _____
_____
_____

• •

WEBSITE _____
USERNAME _____
PASSWORD _____
NOTES _____
_____
_____

• •

WEBSITE _____
USERNAME _____
PASSWORD _____
NOTES _____
_____
_____

• •

WEBSITE _____
USERNAME _____
PASSWORD _____
NOTES _____
_____
_____

WEBSITE

USERNAME

PASSWORD

NOTES

· ·

WEBSITE

USERNAME

PASSWORD

NOTES

· ·

WEBSITE

USERNAME

PASSWORD

NOTES

· ·

WEBSITE

USERNAME

PASSWORD

NOTES

K

WEBSITE _____

USERNAME _____

PASSWORD _____

NOTES _____

_____

_____

• •

WEBSITE _____

USERNAME _____

PASSWORD _____

NOTES _____

_____

_____

• •

WEBSITE _____

USERNAME _____

PASSWORD _____

NOTES _____

_____

_____

• •

WEBSITE _____

USERNAME _____

PASSWORD _____

NOTES _____

_____

_____

WEBSITE

USERNAME

PASSWORD

NOTES

• •

WEBSITE

USERNAME

PASSWORD

NOTES

• •

WEBSITE

USERNAME

PASSWORD

NOTES

• •

WEBSITE

USERNAME

PASSWORD

NOTES

K

WEBSITE

USERNAME

PASSWORD

NOTES

· ·

WEBSITE

USERNAME

PASSWORD

NOTES

· ·

WEBSITE

USERNAME

PASSWORD

NOTES

· ·

WEBSITE

USERNAME

PASSWORD

NOTES

WEBSITE _____

USERNAME _____

PASSWORD _____

NOTES _____

_____

_____

• •

WEBSITE _____

USERNAME _____

PASSWORD _____

NOTES _____

_____

_____

• •

WEBSITE _____

USERNAME _____

PASSWORD _____

NOTES _____

_____

_____

• •

WEBSITE _____

USERNAME _____

PASSWORD _____

NOTES _____

_____

_____

WEBSITE

USERNAME

PASSWORD

NOTES

WEBSITE

USERNAME

PASSWORD

NOTES

WEBSITE

USERNAME

PASSWORD

NOTES

WEBSITE

USERNAME

PASSWORD

NOTES

WEBSITE

USERNAME

PASSWORD

NOTES

• •

WEBSITE

USERNAME

PASSWORD

NOTES

• •

WEBSITE

USERNAME

PASSWORD

NOTES

• •

WEBSITE

USERNAME

PASSWORD

NOTES

L

WEBSITE

USERNAME

PASSWORD

NOTES

• •

WEBSITE

USERNAME

PASSWORD

NOTES

• •

WEBSITE

USERNAME

PASSWORD

NOTES

• •

WEBSITE

USERNAME

PASSWORD

NOTES

WEBSITE

USERNAME

PASSWORD

NOTES

· ·

WEBSITE

USERNAME

PASSWORD

NOTES

· ·

WEBSITE

USERNAME

PASSWORD

NOTES

· ·

WEBSITE

USERNAME

PASSWORD

NOTES

WEBSITE _____
USERNAME _____
PASSWORD _____
NOTES _____
_____
_____

• •

WEBSITE _____
USERNAME _____
PASSWORD _____
NOTES _____
_____
_____

• •

WEBSITE _____
USERNAME _____
PASSWORD _____
NOTES _____
_____
_____

• •

WEBSITE _____
USERNAME _____
PASSWORD _____
NOTES _____
_____
_____

WEBSITE

USERNAME

PASSWORD

NOTES

• •

WEBSITE

USERNAME

PASSWORD

NOTES

• •

WEBSITE

USERNAME

PASSWORD

NOTES

• •

WEBSITE

USERNAME

PASSWORD

NOTES

WEBSITE

USERNAME

PASSWORD

NOTES

● ●

WEBSITE

USERNAME

PASSWORD

NOTES

● ●

WEBSITE

USERNAME

PASSWORD

NOTES

● ●

WEBSITE

USERNAME

PASSWORD

NOTES

WEBSITE _____

USERNAME _____

PASSWORD _____

NOTES _____

_____

_____

• •

WEBSITE _____

USERNAME _____

PASSWORD _____

NOTES _____

_____

_____

• •

WEBSITE _____

USERNAME _____

PASSWORD _____

NOTES _____

_____

_____

• •

WEBSITE _____

USERNAME _____

PASSWORD _____

NOTES _____

_____

_____

N

WEBSITE _____

USERNAME _____

PASSWORD _____

NOTES _____

_____

_____

• •

WEBSITE _____

USERNAME _____

PASSWORD _____

NOTES _____

_____

_____

• •

WEBSITE _____

USERNAME _____

PASSWORD _____

NOTES _____

_____

_____

• •

WEBSITE _____

USERNAME _____

PASSWORD _____

NOTES _____

_____

_____

WEBSITE _____

USERNAME _____

PASSWORD _____

NOTES _____

_____

_____

• •

WEBSITE _____

USERNAME _____

PASSWORD _____

NOTES _____

_____

_____

• •

WEBSITE _____

USERNAME _____

PASSWORD _____

NOTES _____

_____

_____

• •

WEBSITE _____

USERNAME _____

PASSWORD _____

NOTES _____

_____

_____

WEBSITE
USERNAME
PASSWORD
NOTES

• •

WEBSITE
USERNAME
PASSWORD
NOTES

• •

WEBSITE
USERNAME
PASSWORD
NOTES

• •

WEBSITE
USERNAME
PASSWORD
NOTES

WEBSITE

USERNAME

PASSWORD

NOTES

WEBSITE

USERNAME

PASSWORD

NOTES

WEBSITE

USERNAME

PASSWORD

NOTES

WEBSITE

USERNAME

PASSWORD

NOTES

WEBSITE _____

USERNAME _____

PASSWORD _____

NOTES _____

_____

_____

• •

WEBSITE _____

USERNAME _____

PASSWORD _____

NOTES _____

_____

_____

• •

WEBSITE _____

USERNAME _____

PASSWORD _____

NOTES _____

_____

_____

• •

WEBSITE _____

USERNAME _____

PASSWORD _____

NOTES _____

_____

_____

WEBSITE
USERNAME
PASSWORD
NOTES

· ·

WEBSITE
USERNAME
PASSWORD
NOTES

· ·

WEBSITE
USERNAME
PASSWORD
NOTES

· ·

WEBSITE
USERNAME
PASSWORD
NOTES

O

WEBSITE

USERNAME

PASSWORD

NOTES

• •

WEBSITE

USERNAME

PASSWORD

NOTES

• •

WEBSITE

USERNAME

PASSWORD

NOTES

• •

WEBSITE

USERNAME

PASSWORD

NOTES

WEBSITE
USERNAME
PASSWORD
NOTES

· ·

WEBSITE
USERNAME
PASSWORD
NOTES

· ·

WEBSITE
USERNAME
PASSWORD
NOTES

· ·

WEBSITE
USERNAME
PASSWORD
NOTES

P

WEBSITE

USERNAME

PASSWORD

NOTES

• •

WEBSITE

USERNAME

PASSWORD

NOTES

• •

WEBSITE

USERNAME

PASSWORD

NOTES

• •

WEBSITE

USERNAME

PASSWORD

NOTES

WEBSITE
USERNAME
PASSWORD
NOTES

· ·

WEBSITE
USERNAME
PASSWORD
NOTES

· ·

WEBSITE
USERNAME
PASSWORD
NOTES

· ·

WEBSITE
USERNAME
PASSWORD
NOTES

P

WEBSITE _____

USERNAME _____

PASSWORD _____

NOTES _____

_____

_____

• •

WEBSITE _____

USERNAME _____

PASSWORD _____

NOTES _____

_____

_____

• •

WEBSITE _____

USERNAME _____

PASSWORD _____

NOTES _____

_____

_____

• •

WEBSITE _____

USERNAME _____

PASSWORD _____

NOTES _____

_____

_____

WEBSITE

USERNAME

PASSWORD

NOTES

· ·

WEBSITE

USERNAME

PASSWORD

NOTES

· ·

WEBSITE

USERNAME

PASSWORD

NOTES

· ·

WEBSITE

USERNAME

PASSWORD

NOTES

WEBSITE _____

USERNAME _____

PASSWORD _____

NOTES _____

_____

_____

• •

WEBSITE _____

USERNAME _____

PASSWORD _____

NOTES _____

_____

_____

• •

WEBSITE _____

USERNAME _____

PASSWORD _____

NOTES _____

_____

_____

• •

WEBSITE _____

USERNAME _____

PASSWORD _____

NOTES _____

_____

_____

WEBSITE

USERNAME

PASSWORD

NOTES

• •

WEBSITE

USERNAME

PASSWORD

NOTES

• •

WEBSITE

USERNAME

PASSWORD

NOTES

• •

WEBSITE

USERNAME

PASSWORD

NOTES

WEBSITE

USERNAME

PASSWORD

NOTES

WEBSITE

USERNAME

PASSWORD

NOTES

WEBSITE

USERNAME

PASSWORD

NOTES

WEBSITE

USERNAME

PASSWORD

NOTES

WEBSITE

USERNAME

PASSWORD

NOTES

• •

WEBSITE

USERNAME

PASSWORD

NOTES

• •

WEBSITE

USERNAME

PASSWORD

NOTES

• •

WEBSITE

USERNAME

PASSWORD

NOTES

WEBSITE

USERNAME

PASSWORD

NOTES

· ·

WEBSITE

USERNAME

PASSWORD

NOTES

· ·

WEBSITE

USERNAME

PASSWORD

NOTES

· ·

WEBSITE

USERNAME

PASSWORD

NOTES

WEBSITE

USERNAME

PASSWORD

NOTES

•••••••••••••••••••••••••••••••

WEBSITE

USERNAME

PASSWORD

NOTES

•••••••••••••••••••••••••••••••

WEBSITE

USERNAME

PASSWORD

NOTES

•••••••••••••••••••••••••••••••

WEBSITE

USERNAME

PASSWORD

NOTES

R

WEBSITE

USERNAME

PASSWORD

NOTES

● ●

WEBSITE

USERNAME

PASSWORD

NOTES

● ●

WEBSITE

USERNAME

PASSWORD

NOTES

● ●

WEBSITE

USERNAME

PASSWORD

NOTES

WEBSITE _____

USERNAME _____

PASSWORD _____

NOTES _____

_____

_____

• •

WEBSITE _____

USERNAME _____

PASSWORD _____

NOTES _____

_____

_____

• •

WEBSITE _____

USERNAME _____

PASSWORD _____

NOTES _____

_____

_____

• •

WEBSITE _____

USERNAME _____

PASSWORD _____

NOTES _____

_____

_____

S

WEBSITE

USERNAME

PASSWORD

NOTES

· ·

WEBSITE

USERNAME

PASSWORD

NOTES

· ·

WEBSITE

USERNAME

PASSWORD

NOTES

· ·

WEBSITE

USERNAME

PASSWORD

NOTES

WEBSITE

USERNAME

PASSWORD

NOTES

• •

WEBSITE

USERNAME

PASSWORD

NOTES

• •

WEBSITE

USERNAME

PASSWORD

NOTES

• •

WEBSITE

USERNAME

PASSWORD

NOTES

S

WEBSITE

USERNAME

PASSWORD

NOTES

• •

WEBSITE

USERNAME

PASSWORD

NOTES

• •

WEBSITE

USERNAME

PASSWORD

NOTES

• •

WEBSITE

USERNAME

PASSWORD

NOTES

S

WEBSITE
USERNAME
PASSWORD
NOTES

• •

WEBSITE
USERNAME
PASSWORD
NOTES

• •

WEBSITE
USERNAME
PASSWORD
NOTES

• •

WEBSITE
USERNAME
PASSWORD
NOTES

T

WEBSITE

USERNAME

PASSWORD

NOTES

. . . .

WEBSITE

USERNAME

PASSWORD

NOTES

. . . .

WEBSITE

USERNAME

PASSWORD

NOTES

. . . .

WEBSITE

USERNAME

PASSWORD

NOTES

WEBSITE

USERNAME

PASSWORD

NOTES

• •

WEBSITE

USERNAME

PASSWORD

NOTES

• •

WEBSITE

USERNAME

PASSWORD

NOTES

• •

WEBSITE

USERNAME

PASSWORD

NOTES

T

WEBSITE _____

USERNAME _____

PASSWORD _____

NOTES _____

_____

_____

• •

WEBSITE _____

USERNAME _____

PASSWORD _____

NOTES _____

_____

_____

• •

WEBSITE _____

USERNAME _____

PASSWORD _____

NOTES _____

_____

_____

• •

WEBSITE _____

USERNAME _____

PASSWORD _____

NOTES _____

_____

_____

WEBSITE

USERNAME

PASSWORD

NOTES

● ●

WEBSITE

USERNAME

PASSWORD

NOTES

● ●

WEBSITE

USERNAME

PASSWORD

NOTES

● ●

WEBSITE

USERNAME

PASSWORD

NOTES

U

WEBSITE
USERNAME
PASSWORD
NOTES

• •

WEBSITE
USERNAME
PASSWORD
NOTES

• •

WEBSITE
USERNAME
PASSWORD
NOTES

• •

WEBSITE
USERNAME
PASSWORD
NOTES

WEBSITE

USERNAME

PASSWORD

NOTES

· ·

WEBSITE

USERNAME

PASSWORD

NOTES

· ·

WEBSITE

USERNAME

PASSWORD

NOTES

· ·

WEBSITE

USERNAME

PASSWORD

NOTES

U

WEBSITE
USERNAME
PASSWORD
NOTES

• •

WEBSITE
USERNAME
PASSWORD
NOTES

• •

WEBSITE
USERNAME
PASSWORD
NOTES

• •

WEBSITE
USERNAME
PASSWORD
NOTES

WEBSITE

USERNAME

PASSWORD

NOTES

• •

WEBSITE

USERNAME

PASSWORD

NOTES

• •

WEBSITE

USERNAME

PASSWORD

NOTES

• •

WEBSITE

USERNAME

PASSWORD

NOTES

WEBSITE _____
USERNAME _____
PASSWORD _____
NOTES _____
_____
_____

• •

WEBSITE _____
USERNAME _____
PASSWORD _____
NOTES _____
_____
_____

• •

WEBSITE _____
USERNAME _____
PASSWORD _____
NOTES _____
_____
_____

• •

WEBSITE _____
USERNAME _____
PASSWORD _____
NOTES _____
_____
_____

WEBSITE

USERNAME

PASSWORD

NOTES

• •

WEBSITE

USERNAME

PASSWORD

NOTES

• •

WEBSITE

USERNAME

PASSWORD

NOTES

• •

WEBSITE

USERNAME

PASSWORD

NOTES

WEBSITE

USERNAME

PASSWORD

NOTES

· ·

WEBSITE

USERNAME

PASSWORD

NOTES

· ·

WEBSITE

USERNAME

PASSWORD

NOTES

· ·

WEBSITE

USERNAME

PASSWORD

NOTES

WEBSITE

USERNAME

PASSWORD

NOTES

• •

WEBSITE

USERNAME

PASSWORD

NOTES

• •

WEBSITE

USERNAME

PASSWORD

NOTES

• •

WEBSITE

USERNAME

PASSWORD

NOTES

WEBSITE _____
USERNAME _____
PASSWORD _____
NOTES _____
_____
_____

· ·

WEBSITE _____
USERNAME _____
PASSWORD _____
NOTES _____
_____
_____

· ·

WEBSITE _____
USERNAME _____
PASSWORD _____
NOTES _____
_____
_____

· ·

WEBSITE _____
USERNAME _____
PASSWORD _____
NOTES _____
_____
_____

WEBSITE

USERNAME

PASSWORD

NOTES

· ·

WEBSITE

USERNAME

PASSWORD

NOTES

· ·

WEBSITE

USERNAME

PASSWORD

NOTES

· ·

WEBSITE

USERNAME

PASSWORD

NOTES

WEBSITE _____

USERNAME _____

PASSWORD _____

NOTES _____

_____

_____

•••••••••••••••••••••••••••••

WEBSITE _____

USERNAME _____

PASSWORD _____

NOTES _____

_____

_____

•••••••••••••••••••••••••••••

WEBSITE _____

USERNAME _____

PASSWORD _____

NOTES _____

_____

_____

•••••••••••••••••••••••••••••

WEBSITE _____

USERNAME _____

PASSWORD _____

NOTES _____

_____

_____

W

WEBSITE

USERNAME

PASSWORD

NOTES

• •

WEBSITE

USERNAME

PASSWORD

NOTES

• •

WEBSITE

USERNAME

PASSWORD

NOTES

• •

WEBSITE

USERNAME

PASSWORD

NOTES

WEBSITE
USERNAME
PASSWORD
NOTES

• •

WEBSITE
USERNAME
PASSWORD
NOTES

• •

WEBSITE
USERNAME
PASSWORD
NOTES

• •

WEBSITE
USERNAME
PASSWORD
NOTES

WEBSITE

USERNAME

PASSWORD

NOTES

• •

WEBSITE

USERNAME

PASSWORD

NOTES

• •

WEBSITE

USERNAME

PASSWORD

NOTES

• •

WEBSITE

USERNAME

PASSWORD

NOTES

Y

WEBSITE _____
USERNAME _____
PASSWORD _____
NOTES _____
_____
_____

• •

WEBSITE _____
USERNAME _____
PASSWORD _____
NOTES _____
_____
_____

• •

WEBSITE _____
USERNAME _____
PASSWORD _____
NOTES _____
_____
_____

• •

WEBSITE _____
USERNAME _____
PASSWORD _____
NOTES _____
_____
_____

WEBSITE

USERNAME

PASSWORD

NOTES

· ·

WEBSITE

USERNAME

PASSWORD

NOTES

· ·

WEBSITE

USERNAME

PASSWORD

NOTES

· ·

WEBSITE

USERNAME

PASSWORD

NOTES

Y

WEBSITE _____

USERNAME _____

PASSWORD _____

NOTES _____

_____

_____

• •

WEBSITE _____

USERNAME _____

PASSWORD _____

NOTES _____

_____

_____

• •

WEBSITE _____

USERNAME _____

PASSWORD _____

NOTES _____

_____

_____

• •

WEBSITE _____

USERNAME _____

PASSWORD _____

NOTES _____

_____

_____

WEBSITE

USERNAME

PASSWORD

NOTES

● ●

WEBSITE

USERNAME

PASSWORD

NOTES

● ●

WEBSITE

USERNAME

PASSWORD

NOTES

● ●

WEBSITE

USERNAME

PASSWORD

NOTES

Z

WEBSITE

USERNAME

PASSWORD

NOTES

• •

WEBSITE

USERNAME

PASSWORD

NOTES

• •

WEBSITE

USERNAME

PASSWORD

NOTES

• •

WEBSITE

USERNAME

PASSWORD

NOTES

WEBSITE

USERNAME

PASSWORD

NOTES

· ·

WEBSITE

USERNAME

PASSWORD

NOTES

· ·

WEBSITE

USERNAME

PASSWORD

NOTES

· ·

WEBSITE

USERNAME

PASSWORD

NOTES

Z

WEBSITE

USERNAME

PASSWORD

NOTES

· ·

WEBSITE

USERNAME

PASSWORD

NOTES

· ·

WEBSITE

USERNAME

PASSWORD

NOTES

· ·

WEBSITE

USERNAME

PASSWORD

NOTES

WEBSITE

USERNAME

PASSWORD

NOTES

· ·

WEBSITE

USERNAME

PASSWORD

NOTES

· ·

WEBSITE

USERNAME

PASSWORD

NOTES

· ·

WEBSITE

USERNAME

PASSWORD

NOTES

NOTES

NOTES

Made in the USA
Middletown, DE
29 December 2018